TRY THINKING MY WAY

COMPRISES TEN COMPOSITIONS

SATABDI NEOGI

ISBN 979-888569160-4

This book is dedicated to my parents , husband and my younger sister who have always believed in my thoughts .

1.Bhadu& Bhajo- Worshipping Women

There are few ceremonies in India which are women centric. The Indians follow many traditions, Pujas, ceremonies and cultural activities. These are taken as essential activities of life by the Indians. Whether it is right or wrong that's a different question altogether, today I am not going to speak about that.Today's focus is on a special puja or ceremony which is done in the name of unmarried girls. This tradition is called "Bhajo" Utsav .The Bhajo Utsav is celebrated in Bardhaman, Birbhum, Murshidabad and North Ruhr areas of West Bengal.

Bhajo is a festival of unmarried girls. These girls offer their prayers to the God by singing in slokas or rhymes. The term "Bhajo" has come from the month of Bhadro .This is the name of a month in Bengali.

Bhadu and Bhajo are two festivals which are nearly going to stop very soon because of its rarity in practice.

These two festivals are in the name of goddess of Agricultural or crops. It is believed that the unmarried Hindu girls use to worship Lord Shiva a lot, but nobody prayed Lord Indra .So to achieve the prayers, Lord Indra sent "Bhanjoboti"- a divine goddess. This goddess is worshipped as Bhajo Mata.

Bhajo is mainly celebrated by the backward classes girls ,who have no opportunity to study or to work. Bhajo is a goddess of agriculture ,fertility ,work ,education and development.

There is a deep relation between crops and woman. The Indians consider the earth as a mother or a woman .Bhajo is a celebration of women empowerment and advancement.
This type of festivals are there in India and before the totally die off from our society, we should know about their existence.

Today in these type of conditions of the world, where women folk feel helpless and loose their safety because of the ill practices of the society, we need more festivals like these. We are not in need of women power and enforcement until and unless, women folk are given their due respect. Respect is something which cannot be snatched or bought. It is something that comes from your mind and soul. We need to find the psychology behind why human societies had started these festivals. This is because societies have always disrespected women, so to upraise the women folk, these systems are started by our society itself.

Let's try to reflect upon the importance of these festivals and along with these festivals let's start a drive to respect all types of humans in the society, not only the ' Women'.

2. Save Nature And Animals Or Else Don't Bring New Life Into This World...!!

I was watching ' A life on our planet' by David Attenborough a few days back. This is a wonderful documentary which will exactly explain why I have chosen this topic.

David has shown through this documentary how the percentage of natural vegetation and the rate of animals have fallen from the last few decades. This rate has come down to 38 percent in the present year. Just think of it. In this world where the number of human population has increased may fold times, the rate of natural vegetation and animals have fallen to such a rapid rate.

The increase in the number of human population has actually increased the rate of pollution and the land mass, sea, air , sky...every space on this earth is polluted by the human population growth. If this is the rate of increase of human population and the if this is the rate of fall of natural vegetation and animal, then the balance is somehow disturbed. So the world is rapidly going to the direction of destruction.

David Attenborough says that even if there is rise in population there are different technologies through which plants can be grown and animals can be sustained equally. He has even shown the ways how natural balance can be attained even after population growth of Humans. There are many advanced technologies which if applied in a good way then nature, animals and Humans can live together hand in hand and the natural balance can be attained , which can save the world.

But its in the hands of the Humans. If the Humans do not take care of the situation then nature will not stop taking its course. Nature exactly knows how to find balance . And if we do not take care of nature, Nature will take its own care without even informing us. NATURE HAS DONE THIS FROM TIME IMMEMORIAL. Nature has never stopped its course in attaining stability.

And if we do not take care of nature from now on, we have no rights bring babies into this world because in near future there is a question if Human civilization will ever exist. So bring new lives into this world would be foolish thing to do, if we do not take care of our surroundings and Nature as a whole.

So I am greatly moved by this documentary and that is the reason why I felt it important to share the content with you all. Watch the documentary and feel it for yourself.....!!!

3. How working on something gave me some other reward in return ??

I have already mentioned the topic so there is no mystery about what I am going to share now. This writing is for all those people who thinks that if somebody don't give you a job or if you don't go to office or work the formal way, you are a looser.

Is working under some institute the best way of working???

Most of us think that if we have to get something great in life we have to work under a reputed office or institute or get ourselves enrolled under some boss so that we get secured about the money we earn. We have to work for our boss but get the money on time.

Now , in this generation...that is not the only way of earning money. You may or may not work under somebody but you can earn same handsome amount of money. And that's true.

Here 'work' is the word that has to stressed upon not under whom you are working. You can well work under yourself and gain a lot of money. But you have to plan your work. You can open a startup, you can work on YouTube channel of your own, you can work on your Facebook page, you can set up your own business, you can work as a freelancer, you can work as a blogger....and so on. So you can really work wonders if you just make it a point of working and working.

How working on something can give some other reward in return???

This has happened with me and that is the reason I am sharing this experience with you. I have a business which requires everyday work but I don't have a boss. Since I don't have a boss I have the whole responsibility on myself. Sometimes I can bunk also if I want to.

But what I have found is that no matter if I get a sell or no sell , working for my business is important. Similarly if you are working on something else, say a YouTube channel...you have to go on making content for your channel , no matter what.

I have been doing this for quite a long time after I discovered that working is what matters at last. When I kept working on social media, I got my things getting sold. When I concentrated on my business I found my blogging, YouTube channel and Facebook page getting more and more subscribers and views. So its not what you work upon, its the effort that you give, is what counts .....

You work on anything and keep on working. Your work and sincere effort will get repaid in the form of something else. You might get some opportunities in other form...

So your effort on the things that you love to do can make you successful in the long run.....!!

Just keep working. Never get disappointed if you get late reward. Be sure your efforts will repay you.....!!

4.The most powerful teaching of Buddha - Let Go....!!

I would like to share something based on one of the most important principal of Buddhism. But before that, please look at the following questions which needs to be answered before we get into the depth of the topic.

Why we have so much sorrow in this world?

The most important reason for this is that we can never forget or forgive. If somebody has done something wrong with us. We cannot forget the matter and nurture a constant grudge against that person for an infinite length of time.

But what if we let go....!!

Why can we never be happy?

We constantly compare ourselves with others and when we see that somewhere we don't have all the things that our friends or neighbor has, we feel bad instantly. In this way we continue this comparison for an infinite length of time and our sadness continues. And we can never feel happy with our lives.

But what if we let go...!!

Yes, friends. Today I would discuss about this concept of letting go. Whatever be our situation.

When we are angry and are complaining always about our situation or against somebody, we are actually harming ourselves. We are constantly holding a grudge against somebody mean we cannot forget our grief, we can begin fresh.

But that's what Buddha tells us to do. No matter whatever be the sin committed by the other person , its always good to forget the past and just let it go. When we hold a grudge for a long time, we harm our mind and soul so much that we loose all the beauty and charm of our life.

We all are constantly thinking about taking revenge and harming others the same way they have harmed us. But after doing that...do you actually feel good?? or your heart gets more affected by your deeds?? Most of us will agree with me that even after taking revenge they feel bad about themselves. What they thought would do good to them actually took them to a sadder situation.

So when this is the situation. When we don't feel happy even after taking revenge , then why to take such revenge. The best thing is to forget and forgive and start fresh.

But of course we should keep in mind not to repeat the same mistake once again. We should think of the wrong which caused the pain and should decide not to repeat it again ...and just ......LET GO......!!

5. Can we buy happiness for us??

Today, everybody wants some excitement in life. Nobody is happy with a simple unexciting life. There has to be some degree of excitement in everybody's life or else they consider their life dull and boring. This is the scene with every individual in this generation. Nobody can be happy with reading books, doing embroidery, knitting a sweater, listening to music, doing household work, looking after our children and family and so on...

We all need to join the office , earn a handsome amount of money, build a career, grow a social status and so on....Nobody is interested to lead a simple life.

Now I will state 2 examples which will help me to explain my topic.

Case 1

Shweta is a working mother. She works for a multinational company and is married with a single child. She has to put her son in the creche for doing her job. So she thinks that she is not been able to give time to her son. So she buys costly dresses and other baby stuffs to buy happiness for her son. She also buys branded clothes and costly household stuffs to make herself happy. So she wants to buy all the happiness that money can buy for her. But the saddest thing is that she is not happy even after all this. She has got lots of problem with managing her household and her family. She has problem with her job life. Overall when you ask her. How happy is she?? She cannot deny that she is not happy.

Case 2

This case is about Dipali. She is a homemaker. She manages her home and family . She often calls her neighbors for tea or goes to their places for some discussion. She often goes out on vacation and tour and local side seeing . She gets bored by staying at home. She often complains about getting bored . So she induces her husband and other family members to take her to some places for relaxation. So she also tries to buy happiness for herself in the form of recreation and vacation. If you ask her, if she is happy...she will deny that .

Now I have cited to cases where one woman is working and the other is non-working. But both are unhappy. So happiness has got nothing to do with money or material benefits. No matter how much money you spent on buying items or making a tour, you will never be happy . If you do not feel good about your life you can never feel happy. Happiness is just a state of mind. And only doing exciting things in life cannot make you happy. You got to make happiness out of your boredom too. Its not wise to complain about a dull and boring life. Life can never be dull and boring. Its the way you look at life.

Only burrying deep in the online world or doing something exciting or spending a lot of money to buy happiness cannot make us happy. We have to discover ourselves and we need to give ourselves that time.

We can really derive great pleasure from simple unexciting things in life, only we got to feel that way... Its easy and very much possible.. But you need to try .....or else you have to keep running after exciting things and costly things.

6. Why Young Couples Are Deciding To Not Have Babies, These Days?

The current statistics show that throughout the world , young couples are deciding to not have any child . In India also that's the same case. Indias fertility rate has gone down to 2.1.

South Korea is a country where the fertility rate is 1. This means average couples are having a single child . Many do not give birth to children at all. I will give you the reports of the fertility rate throughout the world.

Singapore-1.1

Hong kong- 1.1

Spain-1.3

Italy-1.3

Canada-1.5

United states-1.7

Why aren't women having babies?

From time immemorial, women have been doing this and she was expected to have a child or more . She could only be spared if she embraced the life of celibacy or being a nun.

If a women did not bore a child in ancient days she could be divorced, called a witch or punished.

But today Women are opting out . They decide their priority. They prefer to be child free if they think so. They do not consider themselves as a child making machine.

Fascinating fact about South Korea

There is something very unique happening in South Korea. The youth are carrying on a ' No -Marriage' movement.

In south Korea , the society is conservative and the women are considered to be the sole care giver of the children. Now when they had to work no women could actually manage both household and work. And nothing was done to help them out. So South Korean women chose career over children.

let me give you a data.

The number of marriages in South Korea was- 305,500 (2014)

4 years later the number dropped to -257,600 (2018)

Many women were getting married but not having babies. So they were called Be-hon. Erlier it was not considered normal but now in South Korea it is taken as normal.

HONG -KONG

The fertility rate in Hong kong is also very low. It is been predicted that by the time it is 2041, one third of the women ofhong kong will not have married by the end of their age of child-birth.

Reasons

In Hong Kong women say that they are overworked so they do not have time for babies.

Raising a child is too expensive in Hong Kong.

Educational fees are too high in Hong Kong.

The accommodations or apartments are too expensive in Hong Kong. And an accommodation is a must for a child.

United States

In united states the women are not going against marriage but they prefer to be child free.

Japan

In Japan people prefer work the most. They are giving up the idea of dating and making a family.

China

This country have come to understand the disastrous consequence of opting the one child policy.

What is the role of the government throughout the world

Recently the government is encouraging young couples to opt for more babies, dating and making families.

But what needs to be understood is that, all the governments need to find some family friendly policies, making childcare affordable, making more flexible working shifts for women ,introducing better state run schools and also enhancing maternity and paternity leaves.

7. A Simple Interpretation Of "Addictions"

Now I have come up with a fresh new topic of ' Addiction' . There are different types of addiction that knowingly or unknowingly are followed by us due to several causes... Can you identify what are you addicted to?

I will discuss today about addictions .

Many of us say that they do not have any addiction. For them I would like to specify few common addictions these days which might help ypou to decide if you have any of them.

Over eating, Gossiping, Compulsive lying, over sleeping, Watching continuously television, playing politics at home and work, Continuously working, internet gaming...and so on..

Some people think that only smoking, drinking and drugs are the addictions that we can have. But that is not true. Could you ever think of these listed addictions that you might also have??

We are an addicted generation who are very much addicted to "speed".

We are also addicted to 'thrill', and we are also addicted to ' pleasure'.

We are such a generation that cannot live with simple way of living. We require some sort of excitement in every point of life. We are in need of continuous tiltillation and excitement. We have forgotten to be happy with the simple way of living.

What is an addiction?

It is something which is too strong to be resisted by the brain. An addiction is only a symptom of the inner war going on in your mind.

Fighting an addiction is like fighting with a tiger in the jungle. In the jungle the tiger is too wild to be fought with and so is addiction . Addiction denotes that that you are going through a deep unhappiness going on in your life. Its a way of escaping that unhappiness in your life.

Every addicted person is somehow an wounded human being even if they don't agree.

Think of a time when internet surfing, playing online games were just a fun thing to do . But now it has become an addiction. when did it become an addiction? Can you think of the time?

Let me answer this question. Internet became an addiction for you when life became a struggle for you. When you started facing career disputes and your struggle of existence tried to find an escape.

When you got dejected in life, life became boring and you stopped finding solutions...it is then that you got into the addiction.

Solution for addiction

Let me tell you that every one of you can get rid of addiction. Its that simple. The only thing you have to do is 'to make peace with life'.

You have to feel comfortable with your life without the unnecessary excitements . You have to heal your mind and soul by not comparing yourself with others . You have to engage yourself in some creative activities or healthy activities which will never cause a feeling of boredom in you. You should not always think of money . But you also have to relax and take timely rest and breaks between the various works you do.

If you feel that you are not that interesting as a person or life is boring for you, then think that life is boring and the same for all. Its what you make out of your life. The way you project your life, thats how it will be Never feel low about your existence.

And just let it be how it is. Just try to heal in your mind. Just let it go.. Relax.. meditate and have that constant believe that 'I am not addicted' .

And appreciate the simplicities in your life. .....

8. The Only Bank In India For Poor Women

Now, I am going to talk about a bank made only for the bottom one percent of the women. The bank is made for helping the poor women save the money they earn for themselves.

The most amazing part of the story is that this bank is opened by a woman and is also run by women. This bank is made by a lady named Chetna Sinha.

Chetna Sinha

Chetna has spent her childhood in Mumbai. She completed her education and got a degree for herself. Then one day, an incident made her built this bank for the poor women.

The case that inspired Chetna to build the bank

Once Chetna met with a poor lady who was working as a blacksmith. She was living with her family on an open street. Now to make a shelter for herself she wanted to buy a tarpaulin sheet . So she went to the bank for opening a savings account and save the money to buy a Tarpauline sheet. But the banks refused to help her because she was very poor.

What made Chetna built the bank for the poor women?

In our country only rich people can open a bank account. If you are very poor then there is no way to save money in a bank. Because previously no banks allowed poor working women to open a bank account for themselves. The poor women had no safe place to save their earnings. This made Chetna create this bank for the poor working women.

So she gathered some village women and created her own team and applied for the license for her bank. But since these women could not read or write so the license was cancelled.

Then Chetna taught these women about interest, finance and savings for 5 months and then reapplied for license.

How did they get the license?

When the investigating officers asked these poor ladies to calculate the interest on any principal amount . They could calculate them without the calculator and faster than the officers. This skill qualified these women to get the license.

How did the work progress?

Chetna taught these village ladies how to open an bank account or to make savings account and also to make business. They were taught mobile banking also.

These ladies were assured to bbe given atm cards and digital wallet and they would also get a pin number for that. But the ladies refused to use pin number. They wanted to go for biometric and thumb print.

They said that "Anybody can steal our pin number but nobody can steal our thumb" .

So Chetna told that she learned a lesson from the poor women and that is ' Never to give poor solution to poor people'.

Today Chetnas bank has over a 170,00 account holder and has also loaned over 50 million dollars just to help poor women to make their own earning and make their own savings.

9. One Morning Habit That Can Energize Your Entire Day

The winter season has come and for all of us this is most refreshing season of the year. We go out for picnic and vacation and short trips, fair, zoo, outing and its full of enjoyment.

I have been thinking about writing about this one habit which really energize your entire day. I have been using this tip for a long time and today I would like to share that important tip to you .

Getting up early in the winter mornings is the most thrilling thing to do. Its cool and soundless all around and the best part is the birds chirping and tranquility all around.

Friends, have you all tried to go out early in the morning and enjoyed the morning sun? If not, then just go for it.

I bet you your entire day will be energized and more good if you can go out in the early morning and play some sports like badminton.

You can also do a chatting session with all the morning walkers you meet or your friends coming out for morning sunrise. If you have a refreshing chatting session in the morning under the rays of the fresh sunshine, you are the luckiest person on earth. I do this everyday. And the day I started getting out in the sun in the morning , I feel the blessings of God. I get so much energized that my heart and mind gets full of lively feelings.

Now now that I have shared the tip with you and so I think I should also mention the person who inspired me to go out in the sun early in the morning.

I have some old habits of watching the Doordarshan channel in Bengali. I have yet not given out the habit of watching Doordarshan because of all the OTT s available now.

So one day I was watching a program on Doordarshan, one retired army person came to that talk show. And he is the person who described about the usefulness of morning sun and morning activity.

I cannot thank him enough because after that day when Implemented this beautiful habit of exposing myself to morning sunshine , I could get all the good effects of the sun and all the positive energy just engulfed me from that day.

So friends , in this winter you might not get the time of getting out for a morning walk or activities under the sun because of office or simply because of laziness. But I insist that just try it for once and feel the difference for yourself. And the best time to start this from the winter season.

10. Why Children And Parents Are Getting More Wrestles Today??

Today parents and children both are getting more and more anxious and wrestles . This is something which is increasing with each passing days. Parents complain about their job tension, future of their children and their upbringing . Children are more wrestles these days.

In this blog I would share share some observations of a veteran doctor Dr. Nilanjana Sanyal and her take on this subject.

Why children are wrestles to such an extent that they cannot be controlled?

Today children are seen to suffer from too much of restlessness. They are so much active throughout the day and night that parents cannot understand how to tackle them properly. The main reason for this is that children are not getting the correct field of activities where they can shed out their energy. The entire day is lost in online activities which hardly make them tired physically. So there is a lot of physical energy saved in their body which makes them more wrestles.

Why parents cannot hide their anxiousness anymore?

Parents are very much tensed and anxious with their work life and they are too much stressed these days. They have to think about money, about the upbringing of their children and moreover children are very very wrestles these days. So tackling them is a hard task these days. But apart from these reasons the parents also spent a lot of time on mobile or laptop or other screen. which is also a reason for their stress and lack of concentration. Today parents are also not able to concentrate properly. That's because they are mostly exposed to the mobile screen. Even when they are not working they are frequently checking their mobile for more and more updates. These are the major reasons why parents cannot control their anxiety anymore. Children can make them anxious. But what are they themselves doing to them?

Why is the mobile videos so harmful to the children?

Let me first tell you about our childhood. I am in my thirties so you can guess my generation. In my childhood I used be surprised when I used to get the new books after i got promoted to a new class. I used to love the smell of the pages of my new books. Without anybody telling me, i used to start reading the first few chapters of the new books . Such was the excitement. This is because we did not have the screen teaching us lessons. Our books were stationary objects. But today children learn from online media, YouTube, screen etc. We are introducing them to these moving media . So when you ask a child to concentrate on books, they can hardly do that. They are more comfortable to the motion than the stationary form of learning. So this is doing a great deal of harm to the children. But we can hardly recognize the seriousness of this issue.

What's causing the lack of concentration in children and parents?

Its the same mobile world which is causing the lack of concentration in the children and the parents. They are not able to follow mindfulness. They cannot concentrate on the work which they are doing at a time. Today people are more bend to multitask. This is another critical issue of this generation. Multitasking is actually deviating you away from mindfulness. When you have to concentrate on a single work you are concentrating on 5 more work at the same time. This is creating a serious issue with the parents.

Moreover we are not practicing meditation or sitting quite for few minutes. We are also not teaching our children to meditate. Exercise and outdoor games is a must for children which should be remembered.

Case 1

A child came to the doctors chamber. The doctor told him. " you are so bright and intelligent child , what causes you to be so wrestless?"'

The child answered the doctor. "Auntie...when I ride my bicycle and break all the pottery in the garden , I get some real joyful feelings in doing them.

Case 2

Another child came to the doctor and he was greeted the same way by the doctor. As an answer he told the doctor.." you know aunty when i break the glass crockery laid on the dinning table by my mother, the sound of that breaking glasses gives me certain kind of joy which I cannot explain."

Case 3

The Third case had a reply.." You know aunty, my parents quarrel a lot the whole day. They always go on accusing each other every time they meet each other. I get mad with their behavior. I feel like leaving my house and go somewhere else".

The first and second case obviously are similar and the doctor explains that these children suffer from mental illness, like ADHT and todays lifestyle is a major reason for this kind of diseases. The food habbit is also a reason for this. The food items like pastry, burger, pizza, pasta, maggie, biryani, col drinks, rolls gives a certain kind of instant pleasure to our mind and tongue. These food items create a restlessness in our body. So we should avoid them. Today children don't like to have sabji, roti or other simple food. But these are the food which can keep the children and the adults cool. So food habit plays an important role in our well being.

The third case is the most common case in the world now. The couples are always fighting and that's creating a problem in the mental condition of the children. So more than the children, the couples require a counselling session with the doctor. Today families are breaking each day and these are obvious reasons why children are facing issues with their life in the future.

Children has to lead a very disciplined lifestyle with mediation, games, outdoor activities, healthy food habits, happy parents, healthy neighborhood and surroundings... which needs to be taken care of . And this is not the responsibility of the parents only, its the joint responsibility of the society.....!!!

Contents

Foreword

I , Satabdi Neogi am a B.Tech graduate and am keenly fond of writing . This book is about ten different topics which I picked up from my own diary which I write everyday. I wanted to share my thoughts and ways of thinking through this book. Its just a small start.

Preface

There are many thoughts that comes and goes in my mind all throughout my days. I have been successful in writing those thoughts in my writing diaries. But somehow I have also wanted to reach out to a greater audience. And that is the reason why Iam publishing my thoughts in the form of this book.

Acknowledgements

My acknowledgement is towards my family who have been so patient with me and my thoughts and writings. I am thankful to my entire group of family members for helping me out in getting my thoughts published into a book.

Prologue

I have always wanted to write about Women. So I begin with one of my favourite composition whuich is called Bhadu & Bhajo.

www.ingramcontent.com/pod-product-compliance
Lightning Source LLC
Chambersburg PA
CBHW020855160726
47993CB00004B/1676